CREATING ORDER
OUT OF
CHAOS

**Process Improvement
In Action**

*How An Employee-Entrepreneur
Led A <u>Functional & Process Driven</u>
Re-Design of Security Access To
PeopleSoft® Student Records
For A Leading American University*

IRA KNIGHT

Copyright © 2018 by Ira Knight

All rights reserved. No part of this book may be reproduced in any form or by any means without the prior written permission of the Publisher, excepting brief quotations used in connection with reviews, written specifically for inclusion in a magazine or newspaper.

Printed in the United States of America

ISBN: 9781987712421

ACKNOWLEDGEMENTS

To CD:

A Project Champion extraordinaire – unmatched in your commitment and humility. Without your unwavering support and confidence, this project would never have been possible.

****

To VB:

An extraordinary PeopleSoft® Security consultant and collaborator without equal. Without your knowledge, talent, patience and effort this project would not have been this successful.

If you have any questions, interest, feedback or comments to share, you can reach Ira Knight via::

Email: Ira_Knight@yahoo.com

TABLE OF CONTENTS

	Page
About This Book	7
About The Author	9
PURPOSE	11
BACKGROUND	13
THE PROJECT	15
PROJECT CHAMPION	17
PREPARATION	19
DISCOVERY	21
DATA GATHERING	23
ANALYSIS	25
SOLUTION PROPOSAL	27
IMPLEMENTATION	29
STRATEGY	31
METHODS	33
TESTING	35
RESULTS: POST-IMPLEMENTATION	39
CONTACT THE AUTHOR	41

ABOUT THIS BOOK:

Change and growth are part of the natural and necessary process for both humans and organizations to survive and thrive.

Resistance to change – even when our own best interests – is also a natural occurrence.

Large organizations are wary of major shifts in ideas, innovation and process improvement – preferring the "comfort of the familiar -- even when it's detrimental to its' health and well being. In many cases, this conflict is really the result of an individual (or small group of individuals) whose selfish interests and "power" are threatened by improvements and increased efficiencies. This is a conflict that must be resolved with an answer to the question:

"Does the personal selfish interests of an individual (or group of individuals) outweigh the organization's interests, to the point of placing the organization in a position of vulnerability potential liability?"

It is also vital to note – as important and invaluable as information technology ("IT") workers are, and the incredible value they bring to an organization – it is imperative that a balance is maintained with this "modern priesthood". A balance that reminds everyone that the relationship between an organization and information technology is symbiotic and mutually beneficial – the organization does not exist to serve IT.

Continuous Improvement, not "perfection", is key to the survival of individual humans and the organizations we comprise. This does not mean operating in a state of constant discontent, but of self-evaluation and analysis as a habit and way of life.

In this instance, The Re-Design of Security Access to PeopleSoft® Student Records Project at University of North Carolina at Chapel Hill is just one vehicle that explores principles of implementing Process Improvement within a large institution.

Continue to challenge yourself do the best and be the best individual and organization possible!

Ira

ABOUT THE AUTHOR:

Ira Knight was a Senior Technical Advisor and an employee-entrepreneur at the University of North Carolina at Chapel Hill. In this role he conceived, designed and led the execution of the campus wide project: **The Re-Design of Security Access to PeopleSoft® Student Records at UNC-Chapel Hill**. As a result of the unqualified success of this project (zero downtime, zero rollbacks), Ira has been invited around the world (Australia, Scotland, Singapore, South Africa, United Arab Emirates) to share his experience, insight, methods and roles.

In addition to technical and functional roles at benchmark organizations in banking, software, higher education (private and public) and fiber optics, Ira is also an entrepreneur, publisher, author, playwright, producer, director and public speaker.

PURPOSE:

To share, from a practical, hands on perspective, how a major American public university benefited from an environment where an Employee-Entrepreneur:

1. Identified process weaknesses and potential vulnerabilities having institution-wide impact -- affecting access to student data and work functions of thousands of employees.
2. Conceived realistic, deliverable plan with concrete deliverables and measurable outcomes.
3. Developed practical strategies and methods to implement solution plan.
4. Developed and presented a case to convince UNC-Chapel Hill to:
    a. Acknowledge that a massive initiative and process change was needed.
    b. Prioritize this need for change
    c. Dedicate the necessary resources needed to undertake this project
    d. Properly fund the project effort
    e. Demonstrate the level of commitment and support to overcome the inevitable and natural resistance that comes with large-scale directional shifts in culture and processes.
5. Executed plan successfully. (No system downtime, outages or rollbacks).

BACKGROUND:

Institution: University of North Carolina at Chapel Hill
Location: Chapel Hill, North Carolina, USA
12,000+ employees
29,000+ students

2010: Initial Implementation of PeopleSoft® Campus Solutions
2016: Implementation of Re-Design of Security Access to PeopleSoft® Student Records

University of North Carolina at Chapel Hill went live with PeopleSoft® Campus Solutions (now Student Administration) in 2010. Implementation of Security access to student records at the time:
- Attempted to replicate the mainframe legacy system of access (limitations and all),
- Did not attempt to fully utilize the strengths of PeopleSoft® capabilities and functionality.

The attempt of to mold PeopleSoft® security access in the image of the mainframe system prevented clear understanding of access to student records. A situation that became increasingly unmanageable. Fortunately we were able to persuade the university that "A stitch in time would save nine."

THE PROJECT

**How
The
University
of
North Carolina - Chapel
Hill
Re-Designed Security
Access
to
PeopleSoft® Student
Records**

PREPARATION:

1. PROJECT CHAMPION
2. DISCOVERY
3. DATA GATHERING
4. ANALYSIS
5. SOLUTION PROPOSAL

PROJECT CHAMPION

KEY POINTS:

A Project Champion was absolutely essential to the inception and success of this project.

Without the equity and value of our true project champion, it would not have been possible to receive the institutional commitment and funding for this project. The best preparation, analysis and solution proposals alone would never have been enough to move this effort to the status of "Funded Project"!

CHARACTERISTICS:

- Unquestioned and recognized commitment to the institution's best interests.
- Established track record of success and production
- Trusted for their intelligence, experience and reliability.
- Judgement is respected at all levels: (superiors, peers & subordinates)
- Unifier: able to get diverse stakeholders to understand and buy in to the principle of mutual best interests, not "zero sum", competitive best interests.
- Authority to "green-light"

DISCOVERY

KEY POINTS:

- **Clarity is a must!**
- **What are we getting involved in?**

Prior to considering proposing an attempt to undertake a major, institution-wide project directly affecting the work processes of 6,000+ staff and impacting the servicing of 29,000+ students, it was an absolute necessity to have a clear understanding of the existing landscape and state of affairs.

HOW WE DID IT:

Asking clear questions and insisting on clear answers.
Our objective was not "the pretty picture", but the true picture.

DATA GATHERING

KEY POINTS:

ASK THE RIGHT QUESTIONS:
- *What information and data is needed to fully assess and understand existing security access to student records?*
- *How is access to student records distributed?*
- *Who has access to what?*
- *Are there users with inappropriate levels of access to student data (view/update/correct history)?*
- *How is it determined what users gain access to?*
- *How is access packaged or bundled?*
- *How is access to sensitive data (Social Security Number, Visa/Passport, Special Populations, Grades, Financial Aid, Financials etc.) setup and managed?*
- *Who gets access to sensitive data?*

ANSWERS:
Files with the following information:
- ALL Campus Solutions roles
- ALL Permission Lists comprising these roles
- Full Navigation and level of access for each permission list

PREPARATION: DATA GATHERING

QUESTIONS:
- Where does the data needed reside and how is it stored?
- Who do we formulate a clear and unambiguous request to efficiently receive the width and depth of information needed?
- Who is the custodian for this data?
- Who has access to provide it?
- What file format is needed for data extraction?

ANSWERS:
Files with the following information:
- PeopleSoft tables
- Centralized university Information Technology Services
- PeopleSoft security team
- Spreadsheet format for manipulation and analysis

ANALYSIS:

KEY POINT:
Organizing and making sense of the large volume of data received.
Let the data tell the story:
We did not have pre-conceived notions and make attempts to have the data confirm, we had questions and organized the factual data to answer them.
What does the data say about?

- Distribution of Access
- Inconsistencies
- Redundancies
- Sensitive functions
- Sensitive data
- Inappropriate access
- Blind Spots
- RED Flags

SOLUTION PROPOSAL

KEY POINTS:
Stakeholder Impact:
Why should this be significant to me? What are the consequences for me? The practical answer to this question must be communicated clearly (verbally, written, presentations) to institutional leaders, functional and technical.

The goal was to provide clear and concise information necessary to make an informed and effective Risk-Reward assessment and decision.

- *What issues/problems do we have?*
- *What is the impact on our students and community?*
- *What are our solution options?*
- *What resources are needed for a solution?*
- *What resources do we have?*
- *Do we have the __will__ to solve these problems?*
- *What is the "Best Case Scenario" if we fix issues and the "Worst-Case Scenario" if we do nothing?*
- *Is there a level of acceptable tolerance for a worst-case scenario?*
- *Are there measures by which we can objectively judge outcome success/failure?*

MEASURES:

1. Do we understand the scope of available access to student records?
2. Have we identified and isolated sensitive and critical data access?
3. Are there logical backups for every function in data custodian department?
4. Have all instances where there are functions that only 1 person can perform?
5. Does data custodian department head have the access capability to perform every function in their office?

IMPLEMENTATION:

STRATEGY
METHODS
TESTING
GO-LIVE
(POST-IMPLEMENTATION SUPPORT)

STRATEGY

KEY POINTS:
PHASED IMPLEMENTATION:
Individual Data Stewards implemented first, followed by entire campus.
RATIONALE:
- A. Data Stewards have the highest levels and broadest access to data in their respective areas of responsibility – this allowed us the most comprehensive view of access distributed. (All other campus users would have a subset of this access, not an addition).

PHASES:
1. Academic Records
2. Financial Aid
3. Admissions
4. Student Financials
5. Entire Campus

METHODS

KEY POINTS:

RESOURCES:
Respect and honor the value of functional knowledge and experience
Subject Matter Experts reside in the respective offices of the Data Stewards. We empowered and relied on their guidance -- this provided us with the essential **functional experts** to define and build appropriate access for entire campus.

SHARED CREDIT:
It was clearly and openly communicated that these functional leaders were the reason for the success of each phase of implementation and the overall project – Impossible without them!

TESTING:
We provided environment and atmosphere where they could test and develop their levels of confidence and buy-in to this complete re-design.

ENTIRE CAMPUS:
Mapping of old access to new model.
Fit-Gap analysis and fill.
Communicated changes to affected users.

TESTING

KEY POINTS:
- **SPOT CHECKING IS <u>NOT</u> TESTING!**
- **Audits are only as effective as their methods and purpose.**
- **Finding problems is GOOD testing.**
- **The more focused, methodical and detailed approach you are in testing, the more avoidable problems you find and the fewer surprises you encounter in Production and post-Go-Live.**

TESTING: METHODS

KEY POINTS:
- **FOUR (4) TIER TESTING:**

1. Technical Build (Design/Smoke)
2. Environment Migration
3. Functional (Basic)
4. Parallel (Extended Functional)

Tier 1: Design/Smoke
- Are requested pages/navigation available?
- Do all links on pages work?

Tier 2 - Environment Migration Testing
- Does access function as designed when promoted from DEVELOPMENT to TESTING ENVIRONMENT?
- Does access function as designed when promoted from TESTING to PRE-PRODUCTION ENVIRONMENT?

Tier 3 - Functional Basic Testing
(Environment=TESTING)
- Basic, limited functional testing.
- Is navigation and level of access to each page correct?
- Should access be "view only", "update" or "correct history"?

Tier 4 - Parallel Extended Functional
- (Environment= Pre-Production)
- Are your normal processes functioning the same in both PRODUCTION and Pre-Production Environments, with the re-designed

IMPLEMENTATION: TESTING

      security access?
NOTE: *After Functional Basic Testing, users returned to their daily work functions in their workspace for Tier 4 testing. During this stage, as they performed their normal functions in existing PRODUCTION ENVIRONMENT, they would perform the same functions in the PRE-PRODUCTION ENVIRONMENT. We found, without exception, the units with the most issues (i.e. more diligent testers) discovered here had fewer when we went live in Production – and vice versa.*

<u>Short Term Impact</u>:
- *Reduced efficiency during testing*

<u>Long Term Payoff</u>:
- *User confidence that processes worked with new access model.*
- *No Go-Live anxiety*
- *No rollbacks*
- *Zero system downtime or lost production time.*

RESULT MEASURES:

QUESTION: Do we understand the scope of available access to student records?

ANSWER: YES

QUESTION: Have we identified and isolated sensitive and critical data access?

ANSWER: YES

QUESTION: Are there logical backups for every function in data custodian department?

ANSWER: YES

QUESTION: Have all instances where there are functions that only 1 person can perform?

ANSWER: YES

Does data custodian department head have the access capability to perform every function in their office?

ANSWER: YES

RESULTS: POST-IMPLEMENTATION

QUESTION: Did implementation at any point, during any phase cause system downtime or outages?

ANSWER: NO

QUESTION: Did we have to rollback any designs at any point, during any phase of implementation?

ANSWER: NO

QUESTION: Is University of North Carolina-Chapel Hill in a better position as a result of this project?

ANSWER: YES

QUESTION: Was the project, **Re-Design of Security Access to PeopleSoft® Student Records** an unqualified success?

ANSWER: **ABSOLUTELY!**

RESULTS: POST-IMPLEMENTATION

CONTACT

Email: Ira_Knight@yahoo.com
Website: www.IraKnight.org
Telephone: 1+ 919-627-4554

www.ingramcontent.com/pod-product-compliance
Lightning Source LLC
Chambersburg PA
CBHW030100230526
45471CB00003B/1184